MW01485054

MINDFULNESS AND MEDITATION

21 DAYS TO A HAPPIER LIFE

JESÚS CEDIEL MONASTERIO

Copyright © **2018 Jesus Cediel**

All rights reserved

ISBN-13: 978-1729541432

ISBN-10: 1729541437

No part of this book may be reproduced in any form without the written permission of the author. Digital reproductions are not permitted without the author's permission

Don't believe in anything without question... stay always alert to the possibility that what you believe to be true may not be true and that what you don't believe to be true may be ... but take care that this attitude does not leave you without direction and prevent you from taking decisions and actions throughout your life

J Cediel

Contents

Tell your mind:
I am watching,
I am you and not you;
I can change you,
so you lose your shadows,
and find the light."

J. Cediel

INTRODUCTION

If you are reading this book it is because you are curious or you want to incorporate meditation into your life. To help you to do this, I will show you how to learn to meditate in just 21 days. This period of time is a biorhythm well known by scientists to be especially helpful when you are making changes in your life.

Along with the program I have included audiovisual support material, and recordings of guided meditations, so that you will find it easier to achieve the desired results.

First of all, I suggest that you read the book right through and then read it again, in more detail, so that you understand all the finer points.

The first part of the book is theoretical and the second is exclusively about practice. I will not trouble you with vague, airy-fairy theory; I will tell you only the things you really need to know, the things that will help you to learn to meditate.

In the practical part of the book I will explain the exercises you need to do as part of your meditation routine.

It is important that you do not skip any elements of the program and that you follow each and every one of the instructions. This program is designed to generate a change in your life. Positive rhythms are created only through a process of repetitions that, in the end, become a habit.

I strongly suggest you make a commitment to yourself that, if you miss a day of meditation, then you need to start that week from the beginning. Do not take this as a punishment but rather as the way to establish a routine that, if followed, will bring the best results for you. This commitment must be established deep in your mind, so the first thing you should do before starting with program is to perform a small ritual in which you will represent that commitment to yourself. I'll let you know when the time comes for this.

You must be disciplined to fulfil this routine. Your success depends on committing yourself to 21 days of dedicated work. Mark every day of progress on a sheet of paper or an Excel spreadsheet and do not let yourself be fooled; be honest with yourself, and you can achieve your goals.

If you have any questions or encounter any difficulty, you can go to my website, and click on the *Learn to meditate in 21 days* page. I'll answer as soon as possible. Don't be afraid to ask; other people will also benefit from your questions.

I wish you good luck and good learning for the next three weeks!

Module I

FIRST STEPS

WHAT IS MEDITATION?

The gift of learning to meditate is the greatest gift you can give yourself in this lifetime.

Sogyal Rinpoche

The word 'meditation' comes from the Latin *meditatĭo*, which originally meant a kind of intellectual exercise; while the word *contemplatio* was reserved for a more religious or spiritual activity.

Already by the 19th century, Theosophy used the term meditation to describe various practices of meditation or contemplation from Hinduism, Buddhism and other Eastern religions. Today, the word meditation is the common term used to describe this type of eastern spiritual practice. In this way, the word meditation has acquired new meaning, one that makes it similar to the practice of religious contemplation.

Meditation techniques are as old as humanity itself, but it is in the 21st century, in the heart of our hectic modern lifestyle, that it has acquired special relevance as a means to find physical, energetic and psycho-spiritual balance.

Although there are different types of meditation, I will give you a brief and concise definition. Meditation is a practice of assimilation, which uses the mind as a means to obtain a higher state of consciousness.

In this book you will learn the oriental technique of meditation, but to achieve this you won't need to use complicated yogic positions. On the contrary, you'll be able to practice meditation sitting in a chair, lying on a mattress or even in your bed. You'll see how easy it is.

The goal of this book is to learn to be at peace with yourself and to reconnect with the Cosmos, of which you are an integral part.

This will result in benefits of all kinds in your life.

You will feel connected. Your life will acquire meaning.

Your health will improve in every aspect.

Your social relationships will improve.

You will feel more comfortable with yourself.

All facets of your life will be affected positively by the practice of meditation.

And don't think that it is going to be difficult, since this course is specially designed for westerners.

The course will be practical and concrete, without getting lost in philosophical or mystical ramblings.

THE BENEFITS OF MEDITATION

You must not be swayed by the dictates of the mind, but the mind must be influenced by your dictates.

Bhaktivedanta Swami

When we speak of meditation, the first image that comes to mind is that of a Buddhist monk in the lotus position. And indeed it is thanks to those monks that scientists have been able to verify the changes and benefits that such activity produces in the brain.

To do this, scientists have used modern imaging techniques such as functional magnetic resonance imaging and magnetoencephalography (which registers the functional activity of different areas of the brain).

The amazing results obtained during a study at the University of Wisconsin (USA) with a Nepalese monk and cellular biologist Matthieu Ricard, made in the year 2007, culminated in the monk being named by the media as 'the happiest man on earth'.

In the article published by the journal *Scientific American*, Ricard affirms that through meditation, we have the power to alter our minds.

The study was carried out for almost fifteen years, in collaboration with nineteen other universities, in more than one hundred Buddhist monasteries. Images compared the brain activity of people with thousands of hours of meditation practice, and the scientists came to a number of conclusions. It was determined that meditation has the following effects:

- Anxiety and depression levels decrease.

- Areas of the brain associated with feelings of empathy and altruistic love are 'switched on'.

- It reduces the volume of the amygdala, the brain region associated with the 'fight or flight' response.

- It has positive effects on telomerase, the enzyme that renews segments of DNA at the ends of the chromosomes, and therefore has positive effects for increasing lifespan.

Richard Davidson (Professor of psychology and psychiatry at the University of Wisconsin), also noted that people with a tendency to depression had a greater activation of the right prefrontal lobe of the brain, while people who best regulated their emotions were more active on the left side. Experiments showed that after several weeks of meditation, the left prefrontal lobe began to be activated.

Similarly, other studies have revealed that meditators, in the long term, have a greater neuronal density and their brains are kept younger for longer. It was also noted that the brains of meditators have a higher surface roughness, a characteristic related to the ability to process information.

In summary, it can be observed that all the benefits of meditation come from the reduction of stress levels.

- It helps to relax the mind
- Reduces blood pressure
- Improves memory
- Improves emotional stability
- Improves the quality of sleep
- Improves health in general
- Decreases muscle tension
- Increases the capacity for concentration
- Improves mood

Practice meditation. It is something fundamental. Once you enjoy it, you can no longer stop, and the benefits are immediate.

Dalai Lama

The very purpose of meditation is to discipline the mind and reduce negative emotions.

Dalai Lama

WHY MEDITATE?

As a lamp in a spot sheltered from the wind does not flicker,
so is the subdued mind of a yogi practicing meditation on
Brahman

Bhagavad Gita

There are different reasons for embarking on a program of meditation. This is something very personal.

You may be motivated to acquire benefits in your psycho-physical health, which is more than enough. Or you may be motivated by a spiritual quest, which will give some reason to your existence.

Whatever the motivation, I am sure that in the medium term, you'll feel your decision was right, and it will bring you benefits, perhaps including some that were not listed in the previous chapter.

I want to make it clear that practicing meditation does not imply that you should belong to any religion, creed or philosophy. You don't have to convert to Buddhism. You can go on practicing your traditional religion, or not believe in anything. Meditation is simply a tool that will allow you to get the best out of yourself, and discover your hidden inner potentials.

MATERIALS NEEDED

If meditation was a sport, we would be talking about one of the cheapest sports to play! The only material you need for your practice is a chair, a cushion or a mattress.

Mat or Yoga mat: This is simply a very thin mattress.

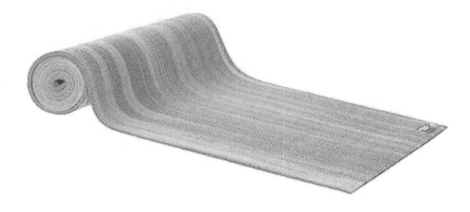

If, instead of sitting on a chair or lying on a mattress, you want to sit cross-legged, in a position of eastern meditation, you can purchase any of these useful tools:

Zafu: This is a round cushion, or one in the form of a crescent, of about 20 cm in height and about 35 cm in diameter that is used to sit on.

Zabuton: This is a rectangular cushion or mat of about 76 x 71 cm that is positioned under the **zafu** to make it more comfortable.

Buckwheat Hull Zafu
has a zippered cover

Zafu

Zabuton

I don't want to engage in any kind of advertising, but I can personally recommend the zafus from Zafu-meditación – they are handmade, and of very good quality.

It may also be necessary, if the room does not have the proper temperature, to use a blanket to cover yourself, since the body cools during meditation.

You might need earplugs if meditating in a noisy place.

A timer or stopwatch with an alarm allows you to measure the time without worrying about it, at least in your initial sessions.

There are timer apps for meditation which can be downloaded free for Android and Iphone. You can download and program them with the time of the exercises in each session.

A LITTLE HISTORY

This section is for those who wish to learn a little about the origins of the practice of meditation. If you are not interested in this topic, you don´t need to read this section; whether you read it or not will not affect the learning of the technique.

The origin of orthodox meditation is lost in the mists of time.

There are some cave paintings, which are believed to be more than 30,000 years old, in which we can recognize some postures of meditation or yoga, but to assert that hunter-gatherers meditated is purely speculative.

On the other hand, the fact that there are no vestiges of meditation practices prior to a certain date does not mean that they did not exist. Various religious traditions claim to have their origins long before historical records began. So it is impossible to know when meditation became part of a religious ritual or shamanic calling.

The oldest physical evidence that shows humans meditating is a seal carved in stone, dated around the year 2,500 BC, found during the excavations in Mojenjo Daro, a citadel in the Indus valley, in present-day Pakistan.

The Indus Valley civilization was a Bronze Age culture that developed from 3300 BC until 1300 BC along the Indus valley, in Afghanistan, Pakistan and north-western India, places from which Yoga, Buddhism, Hinduism, Jainism and Zoroastrianism, among other systems of knowledge, originate.

Meditation techniques were part of the principles of Yoga, and this knowledge was transmitted to a few initiates by the *Rishi* Hindus, also known as the enlightened sages.

At first, these teachings were conveyed by word of mouth, from master to disciple, often in the form of songs or poems.

More than 100,000 lines of verse incorporating this knowledge are found in the *Vedas*.

Around the 6th and 5th centuries BC other forms of meditation were developed in Chinese Taoism and Hindu Buddhism.

In the West, Philo of Alexandria, in the first century AD, wrote about 'Spiritual Exercises' involving attention and concentration, and in the 3rd century AD, Plotinus also developed some techniques of meditation.

The Silk Road facilitated the transmission of Buddhism to other eastern countries. Over time, meditation would move to Japan in the 8th century, and towards the Middle East and Europe during the Middle Ages.

In the 18th century, Buddhism was studied by many western intellectuals. The philosophers Arthur Schopenhauer and Voltaire wrote about it and called for tolerance towards Buddhists.

The first English translation of *The Tibetan Book of the Dead* was published in 1927.

Nowadays, meditation is common theme throughout the world, and it has been shown to have many benefits in situations of stress, for relaxation and health, as well as personal development.

THE PRINCIPLE OF RHYTHM

Everything flows out and in; everything has its tides;
all things rise and fall; the pendulum-swing manifests
in everything; the measure of the swing to the right
is the measure of the swing to the left; rhythm
compensates.

The Kybalion

Your life is influenced by different rhythms or patterns that have been assimilated into it from the very moment of your birth. Any biological, mental or social rhythm causes changes in your life.

A healthy outlook allows you to establish beneficial rhythms or habits in your life, and at the same time to oppose rhythms or habits that produce harmful effects in your life.

To get in the habit of meditating is to establish a favorable rhythmic cycle in your life that, in the medium term, will generate multiple benefits.

To do this you should know how to establish a rhythm or habit in your life. **It is through repetition that a habit becomes established.** It is very simple in theory, but to practice this principle requires a little effort: we must put some energy into it. Once it has been established, you will be able to live, to some extent, from the energy flow generated by this habit, and the practice will be much easier.

So pay attention, because in these three weeks what you are going to do is to generate an existential rhythm or habit that will allow you to incorporate meditation into your life. At the beginning it will require a little effort, and then it will become easy.

To create such a rhythm, it is very important that each and every day, at the same time, if possible, you practice the different meditations and exercises that I'm going to show you.

Once you have completed the 21 day program, you can occasionally take time off from meditation, provided that this does not make you lose the rhythm you have created. But do not lower the guard; in the same way that you establish a positive habit in your life you can all too easily establish the opposite.

While you are creating the rhythm, it is essential to be able to meditate every single day. If for some reason there is a day when you don't meditate, you will need to restart the week from the beginning. This commitment is something which, as I have already mentioned, you will need to commit to before starting the program. I suggest that you make a record, on paper or an Excel worksheet, showing from day to day if you manage to meet your obligations.

This 21 day course is designed to create the beneficial habit of meditation in your life. Do not think that in 21 days you will become an experienced meditator. What is important is to acquire the habit, which is already a great step forward. The rest will come to you with practice.

Remember: Practice makes perfect

CREATING A HABIT: TIME AND PLACE

Meditation is calming the mind so the soul can speak

Jesus Cediel

This material universe you live in is based on space-time coordinates.

For this reason, **the best way to create the habit of meditating is always to meditate at the same time and in the same space.**

There are some people who prefer to meditate in the morning, just when they wake up. This is a special moment because at this time you still have one foot in dream states of consciousness, which will make your meditative experience very special.

Other people prefer to do it at any time of the day, or even at night before sleeping. Whatever the time you choose, **it is important that you create the habit of always doing this at the same time**, at least during these 21 days. To do this, I suggest you reflect on your obligations and daily chores, and decide on your ideal time for meditation practice.

The space is also important and you should always use the same space. There are people who prepare an exclusive room, specially decorated for the purpose. It is not necessary to go to such extremes; you only need to find a small space to place a chair or a mattress. What it is important is that the space be quiet and safe from interruption.

You should feel comfortable, relaxed and safe.

THE POSITION

Without a good posture, there is no good meditation. The goal is to relax the body and make it comfortable. Sit in an inappropriate manner and soon you will begin to feel discomfort in your knees, hips, back or neck. The effect of these irritations will be that your mind becomes restless. And a mind agitated is just what you do not want when you meditate.

Your body posture affects your respiratory status and therefore your mental state. A well-balanced position will allow you to breathe properly and your mind will calm down in a natural way.

It is important that you meditate for long periods of time. It is not a question of suffering in acrobatic positions. You are not looking for an Instagram photo. Forget the images you have seen in magazines and movies.

At the same time, the body must not be too comfortable, since you don't want to fall asleep! **Being alert is one of the essential ingredients of meditation.** You are looking for effectiveness. And effectiveness, in this case, is a matter of calming your mind to meditate.

To this end, I suggest two options: The first is sitting in a chair with your back straight and your hands resting on your thighs or crossed in your lap; the second option is to lie on a mattress. As you don't want to fall asleep when you meditate, if you tend to fall asleep, the sitting position will be better than lying, but either option is valid and you are the one who must make the choice.

In summary, **the position must allow you to have your back straight, to hold still and be comfortable without falling asleep.** You must find the balance in between firmness and comfort.

Your eyes should be closed (although there are forms of meditation with your eyes open).

Once you have adopted the posture, the objective is to remain stationary. Although at the beginning you will tend to move (because you feel uncomfortable or you want to stretch some parts of your body), you must remain stationary. To do this you must learn to relax.

Module II

The PILLARS OF MEDITATION

The practice of meditation is based on three pillars: breathing, relaxation of the physical body and the ability to focus the mind in the right direction.

When you master these three pillars (and this is simply a matter of constant practice) you will observe that the most amazing things happen.

Practice makes perfect

The journey has three stages: relaxation, silence and profound inner peace. And each achievement is built on the previous one. Relaxation is the peace of the physical body. Silence is peace of mind and emotions. Deep inner peace is something that you will come to experience so that you know what I am talking about.

PRANAYAMA: THE ART OF BREATHING

Deep breathing is a simple, yet powerful relaxation technique. It is easy to learn, you can practice it anywhere, and it provides a quick way to keep stress levels under control.

Our mood and imagination have a relationship with our particular way of breathing. The person who breathes deeply always has more psychic and biological energy. The person who breathes shallowly is generally shy and nervous.

Correct breathing is one of the determinants of good health, as well as a balanced nervous system, a serene emotional state and an alert state of mind.

There is interaction between your mental and emotional activity and your breathing process. You might have noticed that when you are quiet, your breathing becomes more rhythmic, soft and slow; when you're tense, the respiratory airflow is choppy and superficial; and when you receive an emotional impact or have an attack of fear it tends to freeze.

This means that **you can influence your emotional states by directing your breathing rates.** If you breathe in a gentle and regular way you will tend to calm your mind. If you breathe irregularly your mind will tend to disperse.

Yogic teachings emphasized that breathing is one of the best ways to absorb energy (*prana*) and to direct it. The suspension of the respiratory process means death. Vedic rishis (sages) say that the *prana* can be stored and accumulated in the nervous system, more specifically in the solar plexus. Moreover, they claim that by using certain techniques, this stream of *prana* can be directed at will by your thought. The yogic science of controlling this energy is called Pranayama (*prana*: energy; *ayama*: expansion).

The conscious breathing technique that I will show you below is based on these teachings.

There are three types of breathing: abdominal, thoracic and clavicular. Conscious breathing is the integration of the three stages in one.

- ABDOMINAL breathing

  When you breathe in, fill up the lower part of the lungs

with air, by moving the diaphragm down and pushing the belly out. You will notice that the abdomen swells.

- THORACIC breathing

  In costal or chest breathing the air enters the region of the chest and very specifically the area of the ribs.

- CLAVICULAR breathing

  Finally, clavicular breathing is performed by filling out the top of the lungs, and very specifically the clavicles.

Each of these three types concentrates the intake of air in a different area of the lungs. By combining the three types, you achieve the aim of completely filling the lungs of air; and, similarly, emptying them entirely.

When you are learning to combine the three breathing techniques, you should first practice while lying down, face up. When you master the technique you can move to practicing in a sitting position. Over time, this technique becomes natural and can be used as the basis for almost any type of breathing.

EXERCISE 1: (Remember to first try this lying down, though as soon as you feel comfortable you can do it sitting.) You must begin by emptying the lungs with a deep breath.

- 1. - Breathe in slowly, softly and deeply, feeling that the air is directed toward the abdomen. Inhale through the nose, sending the air towards the belly. Observe that air fills the lower parts of the lungs and feel how the abdomen inflates because of the push of the diaphragm. When the lower part of the lungs is full of air, you:

- 2. - Dilate the ribs, without forcing them, allowing you to get even more air into the lungs. You can feel this, with your hand resting on your ribs to separate them. When the ribs are separated to the maximum, then:

- 3. - Raise the clavicles, without raising the shoulders, to get a little more air and thus fill the lungs completely. Throughout the process of inhalation air must enter progressively, without jerking, in a soft and continuous way.

The exhalation phase is carried out in the reverse direction, always gently and slowly, without abruptness or effort, emptying the lungs of air.

1) First you empty the top of the lungs (clavicular breathing);

2) Then you empty the chest (thoracic breathing) which deflates and, finally;

3) The belly (abdominal breathing) which deflates until it expels the last remaining air.

If, for any reason, it is difficult for you to synchronize these three phases of conscious breathing, forget everything above and focus only on achieving abdominal breathing, that is to say, inhaling so as to fill your abdomen. The rest will follow. It is impossible to do it wrong if you do so.

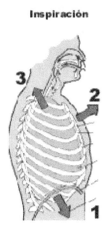

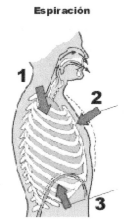

It is important to note that you should not make any noise when breathing. It is essential to breathe silently and softly. Both the inhalation and exhalation should be quiet, slow, continuous and comfortable, without forcing.

All the conscious attention has to be in the act of breathing, so that the three movements of the complete breathing technique are clearly discernible, but harmoniously integrated. Conscious breathing should cause no discomfort or fatigue. In fact, you should be able to exercise as much as you want, at any time.

The foundation of conscious breathing (which is known by many other names), is based on the incessant vibrating movement observed in the universe; nothing stays still. From the smallest subatomic particle to the sun, everything vibrates and rotates. The atoms of the human body are also in a process of constant vibration. Cells are renewed at every moment.

Rhythm is essential in the universe: The beating of the heart, ocean tides, the planets revolving around the sun, and stars orbiting other stars.

Understanding the law of rhythm is the basis of the understanding of conscious breathing. Through rhythmic conscious breathing, it is possible to absorb large amounts of energy and direct it later with specific purposes.

What is rhythmic breathing? The control of rhythmic breathing is taught to instrumentalists, singers and athletes; it is a process that has been used for a long time to raise consciousness to states of trance and to allow a person to manage the oxygen necessary to improve health.

All the teachings relating to the control of breathing are outlined in Pranayama Yoga. Yogis base the extent of the rhythms of breathing on their heartbeats. The heart rate varies with each person, and it is ideal to take it as the unit of measure for rhythmic breathing. The study of yogic breathing is a science and an art that requires time and dedication.

If you want to practice rhythmic breathing, you should focus your attention on the rhythm of your heartbeat, counting 1, 2, 3, 4, 5, 6... until this rhythm is clearly fixed in your mind. With practice, the process can be performed without difficulty.

The rule, in regard to rhythmic breathing, is that the number of units counted to inhale should be the same as the number of units

MINDFULNESS AND MEDITATION: 21 DAYS TO A HAPPIER LIFE

to exhale, while the number of units of retention, the so-called *kumbhaka*, should be half that used to inhale or exhale; but to learn to meditate you don't have to worry about the retention of air. Remember the rule: keep it simple.

To better understand what is explained in this section you can watch the following video on YouTube: Yoga Three Part Breath

RELAXATION

Psycho-physical relaxation is equivalent to a state of tranquility, peace and calm. The opposite is a state of stress, agitation and tension.

Relaxation is the basis of all the work in this program, because your psycho-spiritual internal capacities cannot be used properly if there is psychic tension, and given the connection between the physical body and mind, a detailed and systematic relaxation of the body will decrease stress and therefore facilitate the proper use of these abilities.

At the beginning, it will cost you a little effort, but every time you repeat the exercises you will see that your ability to relax is improving.

The first thing I would suggest is that you choose an appropriate space for your exercises. It is all about creating the right environment to invite disconnection and calm.

You can sit on a chair or lie down.

Make sure that your clothing is comfortable and that there are no objects that irritate or disturb you on any part of your body.

The temperature of the room should be comfortable, never cold. The light should be turned off, and you should prevent the entry of light rays through the window, which can upset your practice, by closing the curtains or lowering the blinds. You must be calm and at peace with yourself and with others, so it is best to avoid doing this exercise if you have just had a discussion with someone or you are excited by something.

Silence is desirable for meditation. Later you will be able to use *mantras* in your meditations. Mantras are sacred sounds that serve to focus your mind in one direction. But when you begin the program, try to ensure a silent environment.

Pay attention to your body, noticing sensations from the outside in. Focus on the sounds, smells and sensations of the space around you, inside and outside the room.

Lying down with your eyes closed, you begin to breathe smoothly and rhythmically, allowing the air to penetrate the abdomen, according to the technique of conscious breathing you have learned.

Focus your mind on relaxing and releasing the different parts of your body, always following an established order to relax your whole body.

Thus, while you are continuing to breathe rhythmically, you will begin to focus your attention on different parts of your body, feeling how the tension leaves these areas and establishes a feeling of relaxation. Take your time: start with your right arm, and then, in turn, the left; then your right leg and then your left.

Then focus on your back, feeling how its muscles become relaxed. Then focus on internal organs, intestines, stomach, etc. You must visualize all of them in turn, until you are finished with the torso. Finally it is the turn of the different parts of the head.

At this point, you should have achieved a certain degree of relaxation, and each time you repeat the process, this will be deeper and easier. Enjoy that pleasant sensation for a few moments.

Exercise

If you have never attempted psycho-physical relaxation before, I suggest you to listen to the recording that accompanies this book, especially designed for this purpose. You can listen to it several times until you become familiar with the procedure. Later you will be able to do this on your own (this is important so that you don't generate external dependencies). Each part of the process has its value in every moment. (15 Minute Guided Meditation. Relaxed Body Relaxed Mind – Youtube-)

HOW TO CONCENTRATE YOUR MIND

The mind is the key that allows you to achieve high meditative states. In order to obtain a high state of consciousness, it is imperative to know how to concentrate the mind; you should become the master of your attention.

According to the yogic texts (*Yoga Sutras* of Patanjali) there are five states of mind. The sage Vyasa lists:

- Kshipta; altered or disturbed mind
- Mudha; dull mind
- Vikshipta; distracted mind
- Ekagra; mind directed or focused on a single point
- Nirodhah; controlled mind or 'state of no mind'

For most people, the mind is usually in one of the first three states (disturbed, dull, distracted).

Of the five states of the mind, the last two (mind directed and controlled mind) are those which are required for the practice of meditation.

The state of Ekagra, in which the mind is concentrated in only one direction, is required to start the practice of meditation. Concentrating your mind on something means to provide all your attention without distraction.

The mind is stabilized gradually in this fourth state, the state of maximum attention on one point. This is the state of mind that prepares you to achieve the fifth state, Nirodhah (or Mahamudra), the state of no mind, in which there is full mastery of the mind and you learn to transcend it.

It is very difficult to explain what it means to achieve the state of no mind, through words; but in short I can say that it is a mind not fixed or occupied by thought or emotion and thus open to everything.

True understanding only occurs through direct experience, through meditation practice. So all you need is time.

It may be that this all sounds a bit woolly and theoretical. Don't worry; the important thing is the practice that you are going to do.

MEDITATION

The Ekagra mind focuses or concentrates on one thing, in one direction only.

Yoga Sutra 1.32

The practice of meditation is based on achieving a state of consciousness in which you become an impartial observer of everything that happens in your inner and outer world: bodily sensations, thoughts and emotions.

This means that you perceive what is happening and allow any experience without judgment, resistance, or effort.

To achieve this it is necessary that you master your attention so that you are not enslaved by thoughts that move toward the past or the future. In a word, you must remain in the here and now: in the present.

To feel and experience that state of peace, harmony, and well-being, it is absolutely necessary to be aware only of the present moment.

And to focus your mind on the present, the key is breathing. You should focus your attention on your own breathing, without trying to control it, in the sensation of air entering and exiting your body. You need to focus only on your breathing rhythm. Different thoughts will appear in your mind, but you should not try to block them. Simply do not follow them, do not allow them to drag you away, and do not allow them to steal your attention.

Over time, you will come to concentrate on breathing and ignore the thoughts, so that you will achieve a feeling of calm, tranquility and serenity.

Said like this, it seems easy, but putting it into practice has its challenges. But I must tell you that through constant practice you get to tame the wild horse that is the mind. That is meditation.

Often your mind is wandering toward the outside, past or future, creating unnecessary thoughts of concern and unrest.

The state of being an impartial observer of yourself and your inner processes allows you to have more control over your thoughts and emotions, and remain more detached from the influences of the outside world.

The practical effects of meditation in everyday life mean that you can enter into that state of consciousness wherever you are, whether you're in a business meeting, on a pleasure trip, in a conversation, or making love. This will come with time and practice.

The true practice of meditation begins when the mind has achieved this type of skill.

When the mind is able to focus its attention in one direction, the other internal or external activities cease to be a distraction.

The person who masters his attention is able to continue with the matter which occupies him, without being interrupted by other stimuli. It is important to note that this has a positive connotation; the aim is not to stop paying attention to other people or to domestic priorities, which would be negative. The mind concentrated on a single thing is wholly present in the here and now, and has the ability to direct its attention voluntarily to people, thoughts and emotions.

When you direct your attention to performing the practices of concentration and meditation then you arrive at the point that leads to what the Orientals called *samadhi* or the state of enlightenment; this is a state of mental clarity unknown to the majority of human beings.

Exercise 1. - Technique to be in the Present

You sit on a chair with your back straight or lie down face up on a mat. You close your eyes and relax your body.

Take several deep breaths, filling and emptying the air in your lungs, without forcing it. You should visualize in your imagination that when you inhale you are filled with vital energy and also visualize how when you exhale you expel all your problems and negativity.

You need to establish a respiratory rate and for that you're going to count the beats of your heart. Count, for example: 6 heart beats to inhale and 6 beats to exhale. You must adapt the number of beats to your own abilities; what is important is to count the same number of beats when you inhale as when you exhale. The number of beats you choose should allow you to remain comfortable.

Then let the breath become natural and focus your full attention on it. Just look at it in an impartial manner. You don't have to do anything, except watch.

Watch as the air enters, as it makes the diaphragm rise, as it exits, how it empties the lungs.

Don't think about anything, no reflections on anything; do not remember images of the past. Focus your attention on breathing. Just observe.

In this way you are in the continuous present, with your breathing. However, your mind will try to take you to other places. Your mind will try to make you think of other things. Each time this happens, and you realize that your attention has been captivated by a thought, you must go back again and begin the process of very carefully observing your breathing.

You must keep in mind that **you are not your mind, or your thoughts**; if you do not identify yourself with them you will see who you really are. But this is something that you will need to learn and experience for yourself with practice.

Exercise 2. - Meditation Technique

Perceive what is emerging in your mind (thoughts, feelings, sounds or emotions) without judgement. Just observe them impartially.

Allow any sensation without judgement, resistance or effort on your part. The essence of meditation is to realize what is happening, complete lucid consciousness.

THE DIFFICULTIES

Nine kinds of distractions come that are obstacles naturally encountered on the path, and they are physical illness, the tendency of the mind to not work efficiently, doubt or indecision, lack of attention to pursuing the means of Samadhi, laziness in mind and body, failure to regulate the desire for worldly objects, incorrect assumptions or thinking, failing to attain stages of the practice, and instability in maintaining a level of practice once attained.

Yoga Sutras of Patanjali 1:30

For any goal you wish to achieve, there are always difficulties. As you begin to meditate you will be amazed at how active, dispersed and sprawling your mind is. Don't worry. You've just made yourself aware of something that happens to the vast majority of people. It is the starting point upon which to build the building.

There is no need to get rid of thoughts. That is not the purpose of meditation, although in advanced states thought comes to disappear.

Rather, you are learning to recognize when thoughts happen and not to identify yourself with your emotions and thoughts. You are learning to understand that you are not your thoughts, or your emotions, or your physical body.

In the same way as a mass of water, agitated by waves, slowly settles again, your mind will calm down gradually. That is why, at the beginning of a meditation, it is useful to relax and breathe rhythmically.

Here are the five classics hindrances of the Buddhist texts:

- Desire: wanting more, or something different from what you're doing at the present moment
- Emotions of aversion: fear, anger
- Concern: accelerated energy, agitation
- Drowsiness
- Doubt: thinking it is not going to work

In addition to mental agitation and emotional challenges, it is inevitable that you experience a certain amount of unpleasant physical sensations. If you're not used to the meditation posture, it might be uncomfortable just sitting still for some time. Furthermore, the state of alert generated in meditation makes you more aware of physical stresses that before you might have ignored.

If the physical discomfort intensifies, you should direct your attention toward something else for a while. You can also change your posture consciously. You don't need to abandon the practice; just discover what it is that allows you to find the balance.

You have to be aware that it will take time and work to incorporate meditation into your daily routine; and also be aware that you will overcome all these obstacles with patience and perseverance.

TIPS FOR MAINTAINING PRACTICE

Here are some tips for maintaining the practice of meditation:

- Practice every day, even for a short period of time. Even if the circumstances are adverse, take this time to seek peace. It is a gift for your soul!

- When you have a small moment, pause in your daily activity. Get in touch with your body and your breathing, feeling the life inside of you.

- You can practice regularly in a group or with a friend. This is a way to overcome laziness.

- Use inspiring tools such as books, or CDs.

- Make a one-day retreat, a weekend or even a longer one. That experience will deepen your practice.

- If you lose the practice for a day, a week or a month, just start again.

- If you need guidance, you can send your question to my website.

- Don't judge your practice, accept what you do and have confidence in the final result.

- Live your life with intensity and veneration.

Module III

THE 21 DAY

PROGRAM

PRIOR TO THE START OF THE 21 DAYS

The time has come for action. It is time to move from words to deeds.

You will recall that I spoke to you of a commitment that you must make with yourself before you start. This is the little ritual that I suggest.

You must go to the place you have chosen to meditate. You will sit on a chair (you can do it on the floor if you wish) in front of a table where you will place a candle vertically on a plate, next to a box of matches.

In the sitting position you will take three deep breaths.

Then, you will light the candle, slowly. Looking at the candle, you recite the following words, or others of similar meaning. To do this you can write them down on a piece of paper and read them. You should feel the profound meaning of what you are saying in this act.

I light this candle that represents my inner being.

In front of it I state my firm intention to carry out the program of 21 days of meditation.

I promise to do it every day.

If I don´t do it one day, I pledge to start the week again.

In this very moment, I promise, before myself, in these 21 days to devote all my energy to improving and increasing the light and peace inside of me.

So be it.

THE 21 DAY PROGRAM

First Week

Choose a day to start. Mondays can be a good start. You have already prepared all the details: the materials you need, the time and the place.

Day 1

Today you are going to perform the following exercise to become conscious of your breathing. You will do it for four minutes.

Exercise 1: Conscious Breathing

EXERCISE 1: (Remember to first try this lying down, though as soon as you feel comfortable you can do it sitting.) You must begin by emptying the lungs with a deep breath.

- 1. - Breathe in slowly, softly and deeply, feeling that the air is directed toward the abdomen. Inhale through the nose, sending the air towards the belly. Observe that air fills the lower parts of the lungs and feel how the abdomen inflates because of the push of the diaphragm. When the lower part of the lungs is full of air, you:

- 2. - Dilate the ribs, without forcing them, allowing you to get even more air into the lungs. You can feel this, with your hand resting on your ribs to separate them. When the ribs are separated to the maximum, then:

- 3. - Raise the clavicles, without raising the shoulders, to get a little more air and thus fill the lungs completely. Throughout the process of inhalation air must enter progressively, without jerking, in a soft and continuous way.

The exhalation phase is carried out in the reverse direction, always gently and slowly, without abruptness or effort, emptying the lungs of air.

4) First you empty the top of the lungs (clavicular breathing);

5) Then you empty the chest (thoracic breathing) which deflates and, finally;

6) The belly (abdominal breathing) which deflates until it expels the last remaining air.

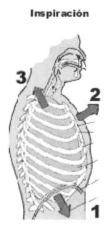
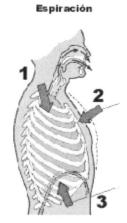

If, for any reason, it is difficult for you to synchronize these three phases of conscious breathing, forget everything above and focus only on achieving abdominal breathing, that is to say, inhaling so as to fill your abdomen. The rest will follow. It is impossible to do it wrong if you do so.

Day 2

This second day you are going to plunge directly into your inner world. For this I have prepared this guided meditation for you. In it you will become familiar with the relaxation method that you will need to do on your own. Don't have expectations. Just do it!

You just have to let go for approximately 30 minutes.

Guided Meditation

Day 3

Today you are going to take a more active role in the process of your learning. You're going to perform the next exercise.

Exercise 2.-Technique to be in the Present

Time: 5 minutes.

You sit on a chair with your back straight or lie down face up on a mat. You close your eyes and relax your body.

Take several deep breaths, filling and emptying the air in your lungs, without forcing it. You should visualize in your imagination that when you inhale you are filled with vital energy and also visualize how when you exhale you expel all your problems and negativity.

You need to establish a respiratory rate and for that you're going to count the beats of your heart. Count, for example: 6 heart beats to inhale and 6 beats to exhale. You must adapt the number of beats to your own abilities; what is important is to count the same number of beats when you inhale as when you exhale. The number of beats you choose should allow you to remain comfortable.

Then let the breath become natural and focus your full attention on it. Just look at it in an impartial manner. You don't have to do anything, except watch.

Watch as the air enters, as it makes the diaphragm rise, as it exits, how it empties the lungs.

Don't think about anything, no reflections on anything; do not remember images of the past. Focus your attention on breathing. Just observe.

In this way you are in the continuous present, with your breathing. However, your mind will try to take you to other places. Your mind will try to make you think of other things. Each time this happens, and you realize that your attention has been captivated by a thought, you must go back again and begin the process of very carefully observing your breathing.

You must keep in mind that **you are not your mind, or your thoughts**; if you do not identify yourself with them you will see who you really are. But this is something that you will need to learn and experience for yourself with practice.

Day 4

Today you will repeat the experience of the day before yesterday. You will listen to the guided meditation. Even though it seems you are learning nothing, your subconscious is taking good note of your movements.

Day 5

Exercise 2.-Technique to be in the Present

Time: 6 minutes.

Go back to the breathing exercise. This time do it for 6 minutes.

You sit on a chair with your back straight or lie down face up on a mat. You close your eyes and relax your body.

Take several deep breaths, filling and emptying the air in your lungs, without forcing it. You should visualize in your imagination that when you inhale you are filled with vital energy and also visualize how when you exhale you expel all your problems and negativity.

You need to establish a respiratory rate and for that you're going to count the beats of your heart. Count, for example: 6 heart beats to inhale and 6 beats to exhale. You must adapt the number of beats to your own abilities; what is important is to count the same number of beats when you inhale as when you exhale. The number of beats you choose should allow you to remain comfortable.

Then let the breath become natural and focus your full attention on it. Just look at it in an impartial manner. You don't have to do anything, except watch.

Watch as the air enters, as it makes the diaphragm rise, as it exits, how it empties the lungs.

Don't think about anything, no reflections on anything; do not remember images of the past. Focus your attention on breathing. Just observe.

In this way you are in the continuous present, with your breathing. However, your mind will try to take you to other places. Your mind will try to make you think of other things. Each time this happens, and you realize that your attention has been captivated by a thought, you must go back again and begin the process of very carefully observing your breathing.

You must keep in mind that **you are not your mind, or your thoughts**; if you do not identify yourself with them you will see who you really are. But this is something that you will need to learn and experience for yourself with practice.

Day 6

Exercise 2.-Technique to be in the Present

Time: 7 minutes.

You sit on a chair with your back straight or lie down face up on a mat. You close your eyes and relax your body.

Take several deep breaths, filling and emptying the air in your lungs, without forcing it. You should visualize in your imagination that when you inhale you are filled with vital energy and also visualize how when you exhale you expel all your problems and negativity.

You need to establish a respiratory rate and for that you're going to count the beats of your heart. Count, for example: 6 heart beats to inhale and 6 beats to exhale. You must adapt the number of beats to your own abilities; what is important is to count the same number of beats when you inhale as when you exhale. The number of beats you choose should allow you to remain comfortable.

Then let the breath become natural and focus your full attention on it. Just look at it in an impartial manner. You don't have to do anything, except watch.

Watch as the air enters, as it makes the diaphragm rise, as it exits, how it empties the lungs.

Don't think about anything, no reflections on anything; do not remember images of the past. Focus your attention on breathing. Just observe.

In this way you are in the continuous present, with your breathing. However, your mind will try to take you to other places. Your mind will try to make you think of other things. Each time this happens, and you realize that your attention has been captivated by a thought, you must go back again and begin the process of very carefully observing your breathing.

You must keep in mind that **you are not your mind, or your thoughts**; if you do not identify yourself with them you will see who you really are. But this is something that you will need to learn and experience for yourself with practice.

Day 7

On this seventh day you are going to return to performing the guided meditation of the first two days, but you're going to incorporate the breathing exercise you performed yesterday during the period of silent meditation.

2nd Week

You have already completed the first week of the program to learn to meditate. Congratulations! Continue like this and I am sure that you will become an expert meditator.

Day 8

On this first day of the second week you are going to do some variations that will allow you to go into a meditative state of consciousness. I propose the following exercise.

Meditation Exercise 3

Time: 8 minutes.

You can relax as is usual in each meditation session. You will see that each time you do this corporeal relaxation you are doing it more quickly. Over time you will come to relax in a matter of seconds. You do not need to do all the relaxation processes that you have done in the guided meditations.

Do the spacious and soft breathing that you did the previous week, filling and emptying the lungs with air, without forcing it. You should visualize in your mind that when you inhale you fill with vitality and that when you exhale you breathe all negativity out of you. So far everything is the same as last week.

From here on it becomes new. Little by little, your breathing is becoming natural, involuntary. Don't make any effort to consciously direct your breath, only look at it. Look at your breathing with all your attention and in an impartial manner.

This time, do not do anything other than observe. Don't count your heartbeats, don't think about anything, don´t reflect on anything, don't remember things of the past, do not imagine anything... All your attention is directed to very carefully observing your breath. Observe how the air penetrates, how it moves the diaphragm, as the air exits ... You're only interested in your breathing. It is the only important thing at this moment for you. Nothing else matters. This is living the present, feeling and enjoying the here and now.

The mind will try to reveal itself and make you think about other things. It will try to get you out of this and take you to its game. It will try to captivate your attention with thoughts and ideas. What should you do when this happens? Very simple: when you realize that you are being distracted from your task, just come back and give all your attention to your breath. Don't worry if this happens to you many times. It is normal. You are taming a wild horse that is accustomed to doing what he wants. But if you domesticate him even a little, the benefits will be immense for you and your quality of life. Courage!

Day 9

The same exercise for 9 minutes.

Exercise 3. Meditation

Time: 9 minutes.

You can relax as is usual in each meditation session. You will see that each time you do this corporeal relaxation you are doing it more quickly. Over time you will come to relax in a matter of seconds. You do not need to do all the relaxation processes that you have done in the guided meditations.

Do the spacious and soft breathing that you did the previous week, filling and emptying the lungs with air, without forcing it. You should visualize in your mind that when you inhale you fill with vitality and that when you exhale you breathe all negativity out of you. So far everything is the same as last week.

From here on it becomes new. Little by little, your breathing is becoming natural, involuntary. Don't make any effort to consciously direct your breath, only look at it. Look at your breathing with all your attention and in an impartial manner.

This time, do not do anything other than observe. Don't count your heartbeats, don't think about anything, don't reflect on anything, don't remember things of the past, do not imagine anything... All your attention is directed to very carefully observing your breath. Observe how the air penetrates, how it moves the diaphragm, as the air exits ... You're only interested in your breathing. It is the only important thing at this moment for you. Nothing else matters. This is living the present, feeling and enjoying the here and now.

The mind will try to reveal itself and make you think about other things. It will try to get you out of this and take you to its game. It will try to captivate your attention with thoughts and ideas. What should you do when this happens? Very simple: when you realize that you are being distracted from your task, just come back and give all your attention to your breath. Don't worry if this happens to you many times. It is normal. You are taming a wild horse that is accustomed to doing what he wants. But if you domesticate him even a little, the benefits will be immense for you and your quality of life. Courage!

Day 10

The same exercise for 10 minutes.

Exercise 3. Meditation

Time: 10 minutes

You can relax as is usual in each meditation session. You will see that each time you do this corporeal relaxation you are doing it more quickly. Over time you will come to relax in a matter of seconds. You do not need to do all the relaxation processes that you have done in the guided meditations.

Do the spacious and soft breathing that you did the previous week, filling and emptying the lungs with air, without forcing it. You should visualize in your mind that when you inhale you fill with vitality and that when you exhale you breathe all negativity out of you. So far everything is the same as last week.

From here on it becomes new. Little by little, your breathing is becoming natural, involuntary. Don't make any effort to consciously direct your breath, only look at it. Look at your breathing with all your attention and in an impartial manner.

This time, do not do anything other than observe. Don't count your heartbeats, don't think about anything, don't reflect on anything, don't remember things of the past, do not imagine anything... All your attention is directed to very carefully observing your breath. Observe how the air penetrates, how it moves the diaphragm, as the air exits ... You're only interested in your breathing. It is the only important thing at this moment for you. Nothing else matters. This is living the present, feeling and enjoying the here and now.

The mind will try to reveal itself and make you think about other things. It will try to get you out of this and take you to its game. It will try to captivate your attention with thoughts and ideas. What should you do when this happens? Very simple: when you realize that you are being distracted from your task, just come back and give all your attention to your breath. Don't worry if this happens to you many times. It is normal. You are taming a wild horse that is accustomed to doing what he wants. But if you domesticate him even a little, the benefits will be immense for you and your quality of life. Courage!

Day 11

You have passed the equator of the course. Today I'm going to give you a break and you are going to perform the guided meditation and during the period of silence in it you are going to incorporate the exercise of previous days, meditating on your breathing.

Day 12

The same exercise for 12 minutes.

Exercise 3. Meditation

Time: 12 minutes.

You can relax as is usual in each meditation session. You will see that each time you do this corporeal relaxation you are doing it more quickly. Over time you will come to relax in a matter of seconds. You do not need to do all the relaxation processes that you have done in the guided meditations.

Do the spacious and soft breathing that you did the previous week, filling and emptying the lungs with air, without forcing it. You should visualize in your mind that when you inhale you fill with vitality and that when you exhale you breathe all negativity out of you. So far everything is the same as last week.

From here on it becomes new. Little by little, your breathing is becoming natural, involuntary. Don't make any effort to consciously direct your breath, only look at it. Look at your breathing with all your attention and in an impartial manner.

This time, do not do anything other than observe. Don't count your heartbeats, don't think about anything, don´t reflect on anything, don't remember things of the past, do not imagine anything... All your attention is directed to very carefully observing your breath. Observe how the air penetrates, how it moves the diaphragm, as the air exits ... You're only interested in your breathing. It is the only important thing at this moment for you. Nothing else matters. This is living the present, feeling and enjoying the here and now.

The mind will try to reveal itself and make you think about other things. It will try to get you out of this and take you to its game. It will try to captivate your attention with thoughts and ideas. What should you do when this happens? Very simple: when you realize that you are being distracted from your task, just come back and give all your attention to your breath. Don't worry if this happens to you many times. It is normal. You are taming a wild horse that is accustomed to doing what he wants. But if you domesticate him even a little, the benefits will be immense for you and your quality of life. Courage!

Day 13

The same exercise for 13 minutes.

Exercise 3. Meditation

Time: 13 minutes.

You can relax as is usual in each meditation session. You will see that each time you do this corporeal relaxation you are doing it more quickly. Over time you will come to relax in a matter of seconds. You do not need to do all the relaxation processes that you have done in the guided meditations.

Do the spacious and soft breathing that you did the previous week, filling and emptying the lungs with air, without forcing it. You should visualize in your mind that when you inhale you fill with vitality and that when you exhale you breathe all negativity out of you. So far everything is the same as last week.

From here on it becomes new. Little by little, your breathing is becoming natural, involuntary. Don't make any effort to consciously direct your breath, only look at it. Look at your breathing with all your attention and in an impartial manner.

This time, do not do anything other than observe. Don't count your heartbeats, don't think about anything, don't reflect on anything, don't remember things of the past, do not imagine anything... All your attention is directed to very carefully observing your breath. Observe how the air penetrates, how it moves the diaphragm, as the air exits ... You're only interested in your breathing. It is the only important thing at this moment for you. Nothing else matters. This is living the present, feeling and enjoying the here and now.

The mind will try to reveal itself and make you think about other things. It will try to get you out of this and take you to its game. It will try to captivate your attention with thoughts and ideas. What should you do when this happens? Very simple: when you realize that you are being distracted from your task, just come back and give all your attention to your breath. Don't worry if this happens to you many times. It is normal. You are taming a wild horse that is accustomed to doing what he wants. But if you domesticate him even a little, the benefits will be immense for you and your quality of life. Courage!

Day 14

The same exercise for 14 minutes.

Exercise 3. Meditation

Time: 14 minutes.

You can relax as is usual in each meditation session. You will see that each time you do this corporeal relaxation you are doing it more quickly. Over time you will come to relax in a matter of seconds. You do not need to do all the relaxation processes that you have done in the guided meditations.

Do the spacious and soft breathing that you did the previous week, filling and emptying the lungs with air, without forcing it. You should visualize in your mind that when you inhale you fill with vitality and that when you exhale you breathe all negativity out of you. So far everything is the same as last week.

From here on it becomes new. Little by little, your breathing is becoming natural, involuntary. Don't make any effort to

consciously direct your breath, only look at it. Look at your breathing with all your attention and in an impartial manner.

This time, do not do anything other than observe. Don't count your heartbeats, don't think about anything, don´t reflect on anything, don't remember things of the past, do not imagine anything... All your attention is directed to very carefully observing your breath. Observe how the air penetrates, how it moves the diaphragm, as the air exits ... You're only interested in your breathing. It is the only important thing at this moment for you. Nothing else matters. This is living the present, feeling and enjoying the here and now.

The mind will try to reveal itself and make you think about other things. It will try to get you out of this and take you to its game. It will try to captivate your attention with thoughts and ideas. What should you do when this happens? Very simple: when you realize that you are being distracted from your task, just come back and give all your attention to your breath. Don't worry if this happens to you many times. It is normal. You are taming a wild horse that is accustomed to doing what he wants. But if you domesticate him even a little, the benefits will be immense for you and your quality of life. Courage!

Third Week

You are heading into the third week and you have already completed two-thirds of the course. During this week you'll probably be mugged by many demons. You will feel boredom, tedium, even stress and discomfort; you will want the session to end so you can do something else. Stay strong, do not desist. Remember the chapter about the difficulties. You might want to read it again.

You are working on focusing your mind and your mind doesn´t like it; your mind likes to be a wild horse, likes to jump from one thought to the next. Look closely at your breath. Try to stay in your center of gravity and not be dragged away by the vagaries of thoughts and emotions.

This week you are going to work a new aspect of the practice of meditation. You are going to focus your attention on the eyebrows, on what Buddhists called 'the third eye' or 'inner eye'.

The third eye is the door to full consciousness, through which one can perceive the world. The third eye sees what the physical eyes do not see. In essence, meditation consists in increasing the power of your perception, clarity and mental alertness. And this is something that does not happen overnight, but through daily work.

Hindus call this physical universe *Maya*, illusion. With regard to the power of the vision of the third eye, the aim of meditation is to exercise this *chakra* (you should work out all the chakras as much as possible to keep the energies aligned and well balanced) to be able to see the real world, the truth, as it is without the mind interfering, with its entanglements, expectations, fears and so on that hinder the real vision, reality as it is.

Day 15

Today you are going to perform an exercise to meditate on your third eye. You will do it for 15 minutes.

EXERCISE 4. - Meditation Between the Eyebrows

Time: 15 minutes.

The last exercise is to focus your conscious attention in the center of the skull to the level of the eyebrows. It is very similar to the previous one, but instead of observing your breath, you just have to stay there, being fully aware of everything that happens, as if your consciousness were a bright sun that expands without limits. It has nothing to do with leaving your mind in the dark and not thinking about anything. It is just the contrary. There will be thoughts. Do not fight against them. Watch them without losing your center of gravity.

You'll find the same problems as in the previous week. The mind will continue to try to rebel. It will jump from one side to the other like a mischievous monkey: it will think, it will judge, it will compare, it will be distracted. You must recall: that is the mind, not you; you are more than just your mind and your thoughts, something more than your emotions and something more than your physical body.

Stay in your center, in your essence, in your being, between the eyebrows. If the mind takes you out, then come back to your place. Again and again. At first it may be annoying but with time and practice, meditation will perform a miracle in your life. Believe me.

From your center, listen and observe how your body speaks with its feelings; observe how your emotions speak and observe how your mind speaks. But do not identify yourself with them. This is the whole secret of meditation.

Meditation Technique

Perceive what is emerging in your mind (thoughts, feelings, sounds or emotions) without judgement. Just observe impartially.

Allow any sensation without judgement, resistance or effort on your part. The essence of meditation is to realize what is happening, complete lucid consciousness.

Day 16

Today you are going to perform the guided meditation and during the period of silence in it you are going to incorporate the exercise described on the previous page: meditation on the third eye.

EXERCISE 4. - Meditation Between the Eyebrows

Time: 16 minutes.

The last exercise is to focus your conscious attention in the center of the skull to the level of the eyebrows. It is very similar to the previous one, but instead of observing your breath, you just have to stay there, being fully aware of everything that happens, as if your consciousness were a bright sun that expands without limits. It has nothing to do with leaving your mind in the dark and not thinking about anything. It is just the contrary. There will be thoughts. Do not fight against them. Watch them without losing your center of gravity.

You'll find the same problems as in the previous week. The mind will continue to try to rebel. It will jump from one side to the other like a mischievous monkey: it will think, it will judge, it will compare, it will be distracted. You must recall: that is the mind, not you; you are more than just your mind and your thoughts, something more than your emotions and something more than your physical body.

Stay in your center, in your essence, in your being, between the eyebrows. If the mind takes you out, then come back to your place. Again and again. At first it may be annoying but with time and practice, meditation will perform a miracle in your life. Believe me.

From your center, listen and observe how your body speaks with its feelings; observe how your emotions speak and observe how your mind speaks. But do not identify yourself with them. This is the whole secret of meditation.

Meditation Technique

Perceive what is emerging in your mind (thoughts, feelings, sounds or emotions) without judgement. Just observe impartially.

Allow any sensation without judgement, resistance or effort on your part. The essence of meditation is to realize what is happening, complete lucid consciousness.

Day 17

The same exercise for 17 minutes.

EXERCISE 4. - Meditation Between the Eyebrows

Time: 17 minutes.

The last exercise is to focus your conscious attention in the center of the skull to the level of the eyebrows. It is very similar to the previous one, but instead of observing your breath, you just have to stay there, being fully aware of everything that happens, as if your consciousness were a bright sun that expands without limits. It has nothing to do with leaving your mind in the dark and not thinking about anything. It is just the contrary. There will be thoughts. Do not fight against them. Watch them without losing your center of gravity.

You'll find the same problems as in the previous week. The mind will continue to try to rebel. It will jump from one side to the other like a mischievous monkey: it will think, it will judge, it will compare, it will be distracted. You must recall: that is the mind, not you; you are more than just your mind and your thoughts, something more than your emotions and something more than your physical body.

Stay in your center, in your essence, in your being, between the eyebrows. If the mind takes you out, then come back to your place. Again and again. At first it may be annoying but with time and practice, meditation will perform a miracle in your life. Believe me.

From your center, listen and observe how your body speaks with its feelings; observe how your emotions speak and observe how your mind speaks. But do not identify yourself with them. This is the whole secret of meditation.

Meditation Technique

Perceive what is emerging in your mind (thoughts, feelings, sounds or emotions) without judgement. Just observe impartially.

Allow any sensation without judgement, resistance or effort on your part. The essence of meditation is to realize what is happening, complete lucid consciousness.

Day 18

The same exercise for 18 minutes.

EXERCISE 4. - Meditation Between the Eyebrows

Time: 18 minutes.

The last exercise is to focus your conscious attention in the center of the skull to the level of the eyebrows. It is very similar to the previous one, but instead of observing your breath, you just have to stay there, being fully aware of everything that happens, as if your consciousness were a bright sun that expands without limits. It has nothing to do with leaving your mind in the dark and not thinking about anything. It is just the contrary. There will be thoughts. Do not fight against them. Watch them without losing your center of gravity.

You'll find the same problems as in the previous week. The mind will continue to try to rebel. It will jump from one side to the other like a mischievous monkey: it will think, it will judge, it will compare, it will be distracted. You must recall: that is the mind, not you; you are more than just your mind and your thoughts, something more than your emotions and something more than your physical body.

Stay in your center, in your essence, in your being, between the eyebrows. If the mind takes you out, then come back to your place. Again and again. At first it may be annoying but with time and practice, meditation will perform a miracle in your life. Believe me.

From your center, listen and observe how your body speaks with its feelings; observe how your emotions speak and observe how your mind speaks. But do not identify yourself with them. This is the whole secret of meditation.

Meditation Technique

Perceive what is emerging in your mind (thoughts, feelings, sounds or emotions) without judgement. Just observe impartially.

Allow any sensation without judgement, resistance or effort on your part. The essence of meditation is to realize what is happening, complete lucid consciousness.

Day 19

The same exercise for 19 minutes

EXERCISE 4. - Meditation Between the Eyebrows

Time: 19 minutes.

The last exercise is to focus your conscious attention in the center of the skull to the level of the eyebrows. It is very similar to the previous one, but instead of observing your breath, you just have to stay there, being fully aware of everything that happens, as if your consciousness were a bright sun that expands without limits. It has nothing to do with leaving your mind in the dark and not thinking about anything. It is just the contrary. There will be thoughts. Do not fight against them. Watch them without losing your center of gravity.

You'll find the same problems as in the previous week. The mind will continue to try to rebel. It will jump from one side to the other like a mischievous monkey: it will think, it will judge, it will compare, it will be distracted. You must recall: that is the mind, not you; you are more than just your mind and your thoughts, something more than your emotions and something more than your physical body.

Stay in your center, in your essence, in your being, between the eyebrows. If the mind takes you out, then come back to your place. Again and again. At first it may be annoying but with time and practice, meditation will perform a miracle in your life. Believe me.

From your center, listen and observe how your body speaks with its feelings; observe how your emotions speak and observe how your mind speaks. But do not identify yourself with them. This is the whole secret of meditation.

Meditation Technique

Perceive what is emerging in your mind (thoughts, feelings, sounds or emotions) without judgement. Just observe impartially.

Allow any sensation without judgement, resistance or effort on your part. The essence of meditation is to realize what is happening, complete lucid consciousness.

Day 20

The same exercise for 20 minutes.

EXERCISE 4. - Meditation Between the Eyebrows

Time: 20 minutes.

The last exercise is to focus your conscious attention in the center of the skull to the level of the eyebrows. It is very similar to the previous one, but instead of observing your breath, you just have to stay there, being fully aware of everything that happens, as if your consciousness were a bright sun that expands without limits. It has nothing to do with leaving your mind in the dark and not thinking about anything. It is just the contrary. There will be thoughts. Do not fight against them. Watch them without losing your center of gravity.

You'll find the same problems as in the previous week. The mind will continue to try to rebel. It will jump from one side to the other like a mischievous monkey: it will think, it will judge, it will compare, it will be distracted. You must recall: that is the mind, not you; you are more than just your mind and your thoughts, something more than your emotions and something more than your physical body.

Stay in your center, in your essence, in your being, between the eyebrows. If the mind takes you out, then come back to your place. Again and again. At first it may be annoying but with time and practice, meditation will perform a miracle in your life. Believe me.

From your center, listen and observe how your body speaks with its feelings; observe how your emotions speak and observe how your mind speaks. But do not identify yourself with them. This is the whole secret of meditation.

Meditation Technique

Perceive what is emerging in your mind (thoughts, feelings, sounds or emotions) without judgement. Just observe impartially.

Allow any sensation without judgement, resistance or effort on your part. The essence of meditation is to realize what is happening, complete lucid consciousness.

Day 21

Congratulations! You've come to day 21 of the program. Today you are going to perform the same exercise for 21 minutes.

EXERCISE 4. - Meditation Between the Eyebrows

Time: 21 minutes.

The last exercise is to focus your conscious attention in the center of the skull to the level of the eyebrows. It is very similar to the previous one, but instead of observing your breath, you just have to stay there, being fully aware of everything that happens, as if your consciousness were a bright sun that expands without limits. It has nothing to do with leaving your mind in the dark and not thinking about anything. It is just the contrary. There will be thoughts. Do not fight against them. Watch them without losing your center of gravity.

You'll find the same problems as in the previous week. The mind will continue to try to rebel. It will jump from one side to the other like a mischievous monkey: it will think, it will judge, it will compare, it will be distracted. You must recall: that is the mind, not you; you are more than just your mind and your thoughts, something more than your emotions and something more than your physical body.

Stay in your center, in your essence, in your being, between the eyebrows. If the mind takes you out, then come back to your place. Again and again. At first it may be annoying but with time and practice, meditation will perform a miracle in your life. Believe me.

From your center, listen and observe how your body speaks with its feelings; observe how your emotions speak and observe how your mind speaks. But do not identify yourself with them. This is the whole secret of meditation.

Meditation Technique

Perceive what is emerging in your mind (thoughts, feelings, sounds or emotions) without judgement. Just observe impartially.

Allow any sensation without judgement, resistance or effort on your part. The essence of meditation is to realize what is happening, complete lucid consciousness.

AFTER DAY 21

Congratulations! If you have completed all the work in the program, then it has been worth it. You can be very satisfied with the work done. Don't worry if you have any doubts about if you have done well or badly. It is very important to have arrived here, having fulfilled the program of 21 days, step by step.

You have created the rhythm, the habit of meditating, which is a great achievement that should push you toward your new stage, the one that comes after these 21 days of learning.

Now you have to maintain what you have achieved. With the basic knowledge you have learned you can meditate throughout your life, with wonderful results. Meditation, like all the great truths, does not consist in complicated and sophisticated techniques, but simply in reaching meditative states. What you have learned is only an instrument (a very powerful instrument!), to reach these states of consciousness. You just have to practice and higher meditative states will arrive sooner or later.

Do not think of the 21 minutes meditation as a dogma of faith. You can meditate for longer or even do two sessions of meditation a day (morning and evening, for example). Everything is up to you. If you practice with regularity and mindfulness you will achieve easily meditative states. You can also consider getting deeper into the study of meditation, either with me or with other instructors.

You can learn to sit cross-legged in the positions of the lotus or of the diamond.

You can also take a course to learn in detail the science of yogic breathing or Pranayama.

If you liked the experience of these 21 days, you will see that it is only the beginning of a long road with endless possibilities.

With regard to the routine of meditation that you used in this course, you will have to adapt it to yourself; with time you will see that the clock is not necessary, although you can keep it.

You will go through moments in which you'll want to meditate and you will do it with ease; and others where it will cost you a lot. You go through your life in the same way as you drive on a road with curves and hills; sometimes up, sometimes down.

If you ever leave meditation, you can always come back to do the program of 21 days. Do not doubt that it will be effective to start again.

Don't forget to watch the videos of the course that are at your disposal. And if you have any doubts, you already know that you can go and ask on my web page where I will answer you as soon as possible

Tantramadrid.es

I hope you have enjoyed the course and I wish you a wonderful life with meditation.

ABOUT THE AUTHOR

Jesús Cediel has spent more than 30 years as an independent researcher.

'The essential goal of my work is to facilitate people on the way toward a state of consciousness that mystics have called by many different names, such as Enlightenment, Samadhi or Moksha. A state that lets you experience life with happiness and fullness, here and now.

Here you can find my personal web page and YouTube channel:

Personal page   http://jesuscediel.com/

YouTube channel: http://www.youtube.com/c/JesusCediel

Facebook: https://www.facebook.com/jesus.cedielmonasterio.5

As you can see I love writing. If you wish to read a book that is different to anything else and defies all you think you know for certain and sure, let me suggest you read *The Verne Code*

 http://codigoverne.com/

https://www.facebook.com/elcodigoverne/

Made in the USA
Coppell, TX
11 April 2024

31156153R00056